Sandra Grant

Bread Machine Cookbook

Table of Contents

Introduction

while utilizing a bread machine for some may seem like a pointless advance, others don't envision existence without newly home-heated bread. In any case, how about we go to the realities – underneath, we indicated the advantages of owning a bread machine.

As a matter of first importance, you can appreciate the crisply prepared handcrafted bread. Most bread creators additionally include clockwork, which permits you to set the preparing cycle at a specific time. This capacity is precious when you need to have moist bread toward the beginning of the day for breakfast.

You can control what you eat. By preparing bread at home, you can control what parts are coming into your portion. It is precious for individuals with sensitivities or for those who attempt to maintain the admission of a fixings' amount.

It is simple. A few people believe that preparing bread at home is chaotic, and by and large, it is a challenging procedure. In any case, preparing bread with a bread machine is a breeze. You pick the ideal choice and unwind - all the blending, rising, and heating process is going on within the bread producer, making it a zero-chaos process!

It saves you huge amounts of cash in the long haul. If you imagine that purchasing bread at a store is modest, you may be mixed up. It turns out that preparing bread at home will set aside your cash in the long haul, particularly if you have some dietary limitations.

Bread machines can make various kinds of bread; rye bread, sans gluten bread, whole wheat bread, and many more. They can also make pizza mixture, pasta batter, jam, and different heavenly dishes.

Incredible taste and quality, you have to acknowledge it – nothing beats the quality and taste of a crisp heap of bread. Since you are the person who is making bread, you can ensure that you utilize just the fixings that are new and of a high caliber. Homemade bread consistently beats locally acquired bread as far as taste and quality.

How to Use a Bread Machine

To begin with, you put the plying paddle inside the tin. When the tin is out of your bread machine, you can gauge the ingredients and put them into the prepared tin.

Later, you only need to put the pan inside your machine, pick the program you wish using the electronic board, and close the top. Here the bread producer enchantment dominates!

One of the main things the bread machine will do is working the batter – you will hear the sounds. On the off chance that your bread creator accompanies the preview window, you can watch the entire preparation procedure, which is very interesting.

After the massaging stage, everything will go calm for quite a while – the rising stage comes. The bread machine let the batter rise. Then, there will be another set of controlling and demonstrating.

Finally, the bread maker broiler will on, and it will steam through the steam vent. Although the typical bread-making process is programmed, most machines accompany formula books that give you various intriguing propelled bread plans.

The best thing about using a bread-making machine is it gets the hard cycle of bread-making easy. You can use the bread-making machine in a full or complete cycle, especially for loaf bread, or you can do the dough cycle if you are baking bread that needs to bake in an oven. To use the bread-making machine, here are some steps to guide you:

Familiarize Yourself with The Parts and Button

Your bread-making machine has three essential parts, and without it, you will not be able to cook your bread. The first part is the machine itself, the second is the bread bucket, and the third is the kneading blade. The bread bucket and kneading blade are removable and replaceable. You can check with the manufacturer for parts to replace it if it's missing.

Learn how to operate your bread-making machine. Removing and placing the bread bucket back in is essential. Practice snapping the bread bucket on and off the machine until you are comfortable doing it. It is necessary because you don't want the bucket moving once the ingredients are in place.

Know Your Bread Bucket Capacity

It is an essential step before you start using the machine. If you load an incorrect measurement, you are going to have a big mess on your hand. To check your bread bucket capacity:

· Use a measuring cup for liquid and fill it with water.

· Pour the water on the bread bucket until it's full. Count how many cups of water you poured on the bread bucket.

· The number of cups of water will determine the size of your loaf of bread.

Less than 10 cups =1-pound loaf

10 cups =1 to 1 ½ pounds loaf

12 cups=1 or 1 ½ to 2 pounds loaf

14 cups or more=1 or ½ to 2 or 2 ½ pounds loaf

Learn the Basic Buttons and Settings

Here are some tips you can do to familiarize yourself with the machine:

· Read all the button labels. The buttons indicate the cycle in which your machine will mix, knead, and bake the bread.

· Basic buttons include start/stop, crust color, timer/arrow, select basic, sweet, whole wheat, French, gluten-free, quick/rapid, quick bread, jam, and dough.

·   The Select setting or button allows you to choose the cycle you want in which you want to cook your loaf. It also includes a Dough cycle for oven-cooked bread.

Using the Delay Button

When you select a cycle, the machine sets a preset timer to bake the bread. For example, if you choose Basic, the time will be set by 3 hours. However, you want your bread cooked at a specific time, say, you want it in the afternoon, but it's only 7:00 in the morning. Your bread cooks for 3 hours, which means it will be done by 10:00 am, but you want it done by 12. You can use the arrow key for up and down to set the delay timer. Between 7 am and 12 noon, there is a difference of 5 hours, so you want your timer to be set at 5. Press the arrow keys up to add 2 hours to your timer so that your bread will cook in 5 hours instead of 3 hours. The delay button does not work if you are using the Dough cycle.

Order of Adding the Ingredients

This only matters if you are using the delay timer. It is essential to ensure that your yeast will not touch any liquid to activate it early. Early activation of the yeast could make your bread rise too much. If you plan to start the cycle immediately, you can add the ingredients in any order. However, adding the ingredients in order will discipline you to do it every time and make you less likely to forget it when necessary. To add the ingredients, do it in the following order:

· Place all the liquid fixings in the bread bucket.

· Add the sugar and the salt.

· Add the flour to cover and seal in the liquid ingredients.

· Add all the remaining dry ingredients.

· Lastly, add the yeast. The yeast should not touch any liquid until the cooking cycle starts. When adding the yeast, make a small well using your finger to place the yeast to ensure yeast activation's proper timing.

Using the Dough Cycle

You cannot cook all bread using the bread-making machine, but you can use it to make the bread-making process easier. All bread goes under the dough cycle. If your bread needs to be oven-cooked, you can still use the bread-making machine by selecting the DOUGH cycle to mix and knead your flour into a dough. To start the Dough cycle:

· Add all your bread recipe ingredients to your bread bucket.

· Select the Dough cycle. It usually takes between 40 to 90 minutes.

· Press the Start button.

· After the cycle is complete, let your dough rest in the bread-making machine for 5 to 40 minutes.

· Take out the dough and start cutting into your desire shape.

Some machines have Pasta Dough or Cookie Dough cycle, which you can use for muffin recipes. However, if all you have is a basic dough setting, you can use it for the muffin recipe, but you need to stop the machine before the rising cycle begins.

Basic Breads

1 Bread Machine Olive Oil Bread

Preparation Time: 15 Minutes

Cooking Time: 3 Hours

Servings: 8

INGREDIENTS:

- *1 cup of hot water*
- *2 cups of white sugar*
- *1.25 ounce of bread machine yeast*
- *1/4 cup of olive oil*
- *2 1/2 cups of bread flour*
- *1/2 cup of whole wheat flour*
- *1/2 tbsp. of salt*

DIRECTIONS:

1. Place the water, sugar, and leaven in the bread machine bowl. Let sit for 10 minutes — melt the yeast and foam it.

2. Apply the oil, flour, and salt to the pot. Do not combine.

3. Set the bread machine to the configuration of white bread and start the machine. (This takes about three hours to bake.)

4. Gobble up!

NUTRITION: Carbohydrates 3 g Fats 5.6 g Protein 9.6 g Calories 319

Preparation Time: 5 Minutes

Cooking Time: 2 Hours and 20 Minutes

Servings: 1 Loaf

INGREDIENTS:

- *1 cup lukewarm water*
- *1/3 cup lukewarm milk*
- *3 tablespoons butter*
- *3 3/4 cups Unbleached All-Purpose Flour*
- *3 tablespoons of sugar*
- *1 1/2 teaspoons salt*
- *1 1/2 teaspoons of active dry yeast or instant yeast*

DIRECTIONS:

1. Load all the ingredients into your machine according to the manufacturer's prescribed order.

2. Program the simple white bread machine and then press start.

3. Remove the pan from the bread machine when a loaf is finished. Shake the pan gently after about 5 minutes to dislodge the loaf, then turn it onto a rack to cool down.

4. Store well-wrapped, four days at the shelf, or freeze for up to 3 months.

NUTRITION: Carbohydrates 3 g Fats 5.6 g Protein 9.6 g Calories 319

3 Ciabatta Bread

Preparation Time: 15 Minutes
Cooking Time: 30 to 35 Minutes
Servings: 8

INGREDIENTS:

- *1 1/2 cup water*
- *1 1/2 teaspoon salt*
- *1 teaspoon white sugar*
- *1 tablespoon olive oil*
- *3 1/4 cup bread flour*
- *1 1/2 teaspoon bread machine yeast*

DIRECTIONS:

1.   Mix all ingredients in your stand mixer but for olive oil. Mix with dough hook at low speed. Mix for 10 minutes. Scrape down the sides if necessary.

2.   Add the olive oil and whisk for another 5 minutes.

3.   The dough will be pretty sticky and wet; this is what you want, so you can avoid the desire to add more flour.

4.   Put the dough on a kindly floured surface, cover it with a large bowl or oily plastic wrap, then leave it for 15 minutes.

5.   Dust Baking sheets with light flour, or cover them with parchment paper.

6.   Divide the dough into two parts using a serrated knife and shape each piece into a 3×14-inch oval.

7.   Place the loaves on prepared sheets and dust with flour.

8.   Cover the dough loaves and leave them to rise for about 45 minutes at a draft-free spot.

9.   Preheat bread machine to 425 F.

10.   Spritz loaves with water.

11.   Put the bread on the middle rack of the bread machine.

12.   Bake, for approximately 25 to 35 mins, until its color is golden brown.

13.   Serve and have fun.

NUTRITION: Carbohydrates 3 g Fats 5.6 g Protein 9.6 g Calories 319

4   Crusty French Bread

Prep Time: 10 Minutes
Total Time: 3 hours 35 minutes

INGREDIENTS:

1 teaspoon Instant yeast
1 and a half teaspoons of sugar
1 cup Lukewarm water
1 and a half teaspoons salt
1 and a half teaspoons of butter
3 cups Bread flour
Glaze:
1 teaspoon water
One egg white

DIRECTIONS:

Add all the Ingredients to the bread
machine as per your machine's suggested
order.
Select the dough cycle. Adjust the consistency of
dough after 5 to 10 minutes by adding one tbsp. of
water at a time for very dry dough or one tbsp. of flour
if it's
too sticky.
It should pull away after sticking to the
sides.
After the machine is done, take out the dough on a
clean, floured surface. Shape into cylinder shape
loaves. Shape into French bread.

Place the loaves in oiled baking pans.

Cover with a towel and let it rise in a warm place.

Let the oven preheat to 425 F. make the glaze by mixing water with egg.

Coat the loaf's surface with a glaze.

Make cuts onto the dough surface.

Bake in the oven for 20 minutes.

Lower the oven's temperature to 350 F, bake for 5 to 10 minutes more or until golden brown.

Check the bread's internal temperature. It should be 195 F.

Cool slightly and serve fresh.

NUTRITION: Calories: 180 Carbs: 28 g   Fat: 3 g Protein: 6 g

5 Everyday White Bread

(Prep time: 20 minutes | Total time: 2 hours 30 minutes)

INGREDIENTS

3 and 3/4 cups of flour
Lukewarm water 1 cup
Butter 3 tbsp.
Lukewarm milk 1/3 cup
Bread machine Yeast 2 tsp
Sugar 3 tbsp.
Salt 1 tsp

DIRECTIONS:

In the bread machine, add all the ingredients according to your machine's order.

Select 2 pounds' loaf, and basic setting, medium crust. Click on start.

After it's baked, let it cool down before slicing.

NUTRITION: Calories: 78 Carbs: 11 g   Fat: 1 g Protein: 2 g

6 Extra Buttery White Bread

Prep Time: 10 Minutes
Cook Time: 3 hours 10 minutes

INGREDIENTS:

1⅛ cups milk
4 Tbsp unsalted butter
3 cups bread flour
1½ Tbsp white granulated sugar
1½ tsp salt
1½ tsp bread machine yeast

DIRECTIONS:

1. Soften the butter in your microwave.
2. Add each ingredient to the bread machine in the order and at the temperature recommended by your bread machine manufacturer.
3. Close the lid, select the basic or white bread, medium crust setting on your bread machine, and press start.
4. When the bread machine has finished baking, remove the bread and put it on a cooling rack.

NUTRITION: Carbs: 22 g   Fat: 1 g   Protein: 4 g
Calories: 104

7 Honey Whole-Wheat Bread

(Prep time: 5 minutes | Total time: 3 hours 30 minutes)

Ingredients

Olive oil: ⅓ cup
4 and a half cups of whole wheat flour
1 and a half cups of warm water
Honey: ⅓ cup
Yeast: 1 tablespoon
Kosher salt: 2 tsp
Gluten: 1 tsp (optional)

DIRECTIONS:

In the machine, add water, then oil, and then honey.

Add half flour, salt, gluten, and the rest of the flour.

Make a well in the center add yeast.

Select whole wheat and light crust. Press start.

Serve fresh bread.

NUTRITION: Calories: 199 Cal Carbs: 37 g Fat: 4.2 g Protein: 6.2 g

8 Light Sourdough Bread

Preparation Time: 5 Minutes

Cooking Time: 25 Minutes

Servings: 8

INGREDIENTS:

Sourdough starter:

- *1 1/2 cups of water*
- *2 cups (256 grams) of bread flour*
- *2 tsp. of active dry yeast*

Bread ingredients:

- *3 tbsp. of apple cider vinegar*
- *2 tbsp. of lemon juice*
- *3 cups of bread flour*
- *1 tsp. of fine sea salt*
- *2 tsp. of active dry yeast*

DIRECTIONS:

1. Put the kneading blades in the bread machine; Place the pan of bread into the machine.

2. Add the bread flour and leaven in the bowl.

3. Set a "sourdough starter" course and press Start. It will take around 2 hours to complete.

4. The starting point is all bubbly.

For the bread:

5. Hit cancel to clear once the sourdough starter ends and beeps.

6. Add in the specified ingredients, with yeast placed on top of the flour.

7.   Close the cover and set a "basic" sequence.

8.   When the bread is baked (just 4 hours), pop out and knock out onto a cooling rack.

9.   When cooled, the bread can be cut and frozen for a long time storage.

NUTRITION: Carbohydrates 3 g Fats 5.6 g Protein 9.6 g Calories 319

(Prep time: 10 minutes | Total time: 4 hours 10 minutes)

Ingredients

Whole wheat flour: 1 and 3⁄4 cups

Water: 3⁄4 cup

Melted butter: 3 tablespoons

Milk: 1⁄3 cup

Sugar: 2 tablespoons

Molasses: 3 tablespoons

Fast-rising yeast: 2 and 1⁄4 teaspoons

Bread flour: 2 cups

Salt: 1 teaspoon

DIRECTIONS:

Add all the ingredients to the machine according to your suggested machine's order. Make sure the ingredients are at room temperature

Use light crust, basic setting.

Serve fresh.

NUTRITION: Calories: 164 Cal Fat: 2 g Carbs: 34 g Protein: 4 g

Preparation Time: 15 Minutes

Cooking Time: 3 Hours and 20 Minutes

Servings: 8

INGREDIENTS:

- *1 cup of lukewarm (105 to 115 degrees F/40 to 45 degrees C)*
- *4 teaspoons of honey*
- *2 teaspoons of active dry yeast*
- *2 cups of all-purpose flour*
- *4 teaspoons of olive oil*
- *1/2 teaspoon of salt*

DIRECTIONS:

1. Put warm water into the bread machine pan and sprinkle honey in warm water until honey is dissolved. Add yeast to the mixture and let it sit for about 10 minutes before yeast begins to foam. In the manufacturer's suggested order, add flour, olive oil, and salt to the bread pan.

2. If the machine has that choice, select a soft setting; otherwise, set a standard-setting, and start the machine. Let the bread cool before slicing.

NUTRITION: Carbohydrates 3 g Fats 5.6 g Protein 9.6 g Calories 319

Prep Time: 5 Minutes
Cook Time: 3 hours

INGREDIENTS:

1⅓ cups water
⅓ cup plant milk (I use silk soy original)
1½ tsp salt
2 Tbsp granulated sugar
2 Tbsp vegetable oil
3½ cups all-purpose flour
1¾ tsp bread machine yeast

DIRECTIONS:

1. Add each ingredient to the bread machine in the order and at the temperature recommended by your bread machine manufacturer.

2. Close the lid, select the basic or white bread, medium crust setting on your bread machine, and press start.

3. When the bread machine has finished baking, remove the bread and put it on a cooling rack.

NUTRITION: Carbs: 13 g   Fat: 2 g   Protein: 3 g Calories: 80

12 Whole-Wheat Bread

(Prep time: 10 minutes | Total time: 4 hours 10 minutes)

Ingredients

3 and 1/3 cups of whole wheat flour

2 tablespoons Powdered milk

1 and a half cups of water

2 tablespoons Honey

2 tablespoons Molasses

2 tablespoons Margarine

Salt: 1 and a half teaspoons

Yeast: 1 and a half teaspoons

DIRECTIONS:

Add liquid ingredients before dry ingredients or as per your machine's order.

Mix the powdered milk and water. Heat in microwave for 30 seconds, then adds in the bread machine followed by rest of the ingredients.

Select 2 lb. loaf and whole wheat bread press start. Serve fresh.

NUTRITION: Calories: 196 Cal Carbs: 36.8g Fat: 3.89 g Protein: 6.42g

Vegetable Bread

13 Beetroot Prune Bread

Preparation Time: 3 hours
Cooking Time: 30 minutes
Servings: 20

INGREDIENTS:

- *1½ cups lukewarm beet broth*
- *5¼ cups all-purpose flour*
- *1 cup beet puree*
- *1 cup prunes, chopped*
- *3 tablespoons extra virgin olive oil*
- *5 tablespoons dry cream*
- *1 tablespoon brown sugar*
- *2 teaspoons active dry yeast*
- *1 tablespoon whole milk*
- *3 teaspoons sea salt*

DIRECTIONS:

1   Prepare all of the ingredients for your bread and measuring means (a cup, a spoon, kitchen scales).

2   Carefully measure the ingredients into the pan, except the prunes.

3   Place all of the ingredients into the bread bucket in the right order, following the manual for your bread machine.

4   Close the cover.

5   Select the program of your bread machine to BASIC and choose the crust color to medium.

6   Press START.

7   After the signal, put the prunes to the dough.

8   Wait until the program completes.

9   When done, take the bucket out and let it cool for 5-10 minutes.

10 Shake the loaf from the pan and let cool for 30 minutes on a cooling rack.

11 Slice, serve, and enjoy the taste of fragrant homemade bread.

NUTRITION: Calories: 443 calories; Total Carbohydrate: 81.1 g Total Fat: 8.2 g Protein: 9.9 g Sodium: 604 mg Fiber: 4.4 g Sugar: 11.7 g

Preparation Time: 2 hours 20 minutes

Cooking time: 50 minutes

Servings: 1 loaf

INGREDIENTS:

- *¼ cup of water*
- *4 tablespoons olive oil*
- *1 egg white*
- *1 teaspoon lemon juice*
- *2/3 cup grated cheddar cheese*
- *3 tablespoons green onion*
- *½ cup broccoli, chopped*
- *½ cup cauliflower, chopped*
- *½ teaspoon lemon pepper seasoning*
- *2 cups bread flour*
- *1 teaspoon bread machine yeast*

DIRECTIONS:

1.   Put all fixings into your bread machine, carefully following the directions of the manufacturer

2.   Set the program of your bread machine to Basic/White Bread and set crust type to Medium. Press starts.

3.   Wait until the cycle completes. Once the loaf is ready, take the bucket out and let the loaf cool within 5 minutes. Shake the bucket to remove the loaf. Transfer, slice, and serve.

NUTRITION: Calories: 156 Fat: 8 g Carbohydrates: 17 g Protein: 5 g

15 Celery Loaf

Preparation Time: 2 hours 40 minutes
Cooking time: 50 minutes
Servings: 1 loaf

INGREDIENTS:

- *1 can (10 ounces) cream of celery soup*
- *3 tablespoons low-fat milk, heated*
- *1 tablespoon vegetable oil*
- *1¼ teaspoons celery salt*
- *¾ cup celery, fresh/sliced thin*
- *1 tablespoon celery leaves, fresh, chopped*
- *1 whole egg*
- *¼ teaspoon sugar*
- *3 cups bread flour*
- *¼ teaspoon ginger*
- *½ cup quick-cooking oats*
- *2 tablespoons gluten*
- *2 teaspoons celery seeds*
- *1 pack of active dry yeast*

DIRECTIONS:

1.   Put all of the fixings into your bread machine, carefully following the directions of the manufacturer.

2.   Set the program of your bread machine to Basic/White Bread and set crust type to Medium. Press starts.

3.   Wait until the cycle completes. Once the loaf is ready, take the bucket out and let the loaf cool within 5 minutes. Shake the bucket to remove the loaf. Transfer, slice, and serve.

NUTRITION: Calories: 73 Fat: 4 g Carbohydrates: 8 g Protein: 3 g

16 Curd Bread

Preparation Time: 4 hours
Cooking Time: 15 minutes
Servings: 12

INGREDIENTS:

- *¾ cup lukewarm water*
- *2/3 cups wheat bread machine flour*
- *¾ cup cottage cheese*
- *2 Tablespoon softened butter*
- *Tablespoon white sugar*
- *1½ teaspoon sea salt*
- *1½ Tablespoon sesame seeds*
- *2 Tablespoon dried onions*
- *1¼ teaspoon bread machine yeast*

DIRECTIONS:

2   Place all the dry and liquid ingredients in the pan and follow the directions for your bread machine.

3   Pay particular attention to measuring the ingredients. Use a measuring cup, measuring spoon, and kitchen scales to do so.

4   Set the baking program to BASIC and the crust type to MEDIUM.

5   If the dough is too dense or too wet, adjust the amount of flour and liquid in the recipe.

6   When the program has ended, take the pan out of the bread machine and let it cool for 5 minutes.

7   Shake the loaf out of the pan. If necessary, use a spatula.

8   Wrap the bread with a kitchen towel and set it aside for an hour. Otherwise, you can cool it on a wire rack.

NUTRITION: Calories: 277 calories; Total Carbohydrate: 48.4 g Total Fat: 4.7g Protein: 9.4 g

17 Curvy Carrot Bread

Preparation Time: 2 hours
Cooking Time: 15 minutes
Servings: 12

INGREDIENTS:

- ¾ cup milk, lukewarm
- 3 tablespoons butter, melted at room temperature
- 1 tablespoon honey
- ¾ teaspoon ground nutmeg
- ½ teaspoon salt
- 1 ½ cups shredded carrot
- 3 cups white bread flour
- ¼ teaspoons bread machine or active dry yeast

DIRECTIONS:

1   Take 1 ½ pound size loaf pan and first add the liquid ingredients and then add the dry ingredients.

2   Place the loaf pan in the machine and close its top lid.

3   Plug the bread machine into power socket. For selecting a bread cycle, press "Quick Bread/Rapid Bread" and for selecting a crust type, press "Light" or "Medium".

4   Start the machine, and it will start preparing the bread.

5   After the bread loaf is completed, open the lid and take out the loaf pan.

6   Allow the pan to cool down for 10-15 minutes on a wire rack. Gently shake the pan and remove the bread loaf.

7   Make slices and serve.

NUTRITION: Calories: 142 calories; Total Carbohydrate: 32.2 g Total Fat: 0.8 g Protein: 2.33 g

18 Potato Bread

Preparation Time: 3 hours

Cooking time: 45 minutes

Servings: 2 loaves

INGREDIENTS:

- *1 3/4 teaspoon active dry yeast*
- *2 tablespoon dry milk*
- *1/4 cup instant potato flakes*
- *2 tablespoon sugar*
- *4 cups bread flour*
- *1 1/4 teaspoon salt*
- *2 tablespoon butter*
- *1 3/8 cups water*

DIRECTIONS:

1.   Put all the liquid ingredients in the pan. Add all the dry ingredients, except the yeast. Form a shallow hole in the middle of the dry ingredients and place the yeast.

2.   Secure the pan in the machine and close the lid. Choose the basic setting and your desired color of the crust. Press starts. Allow the bread to cool before slicing.

NUTRITION: Calories: 35 Carbohydrate: 19 g Fat: 0 g Protein: 4 g

Preparation Time: 1 hour 20 minutes
Cooking time: 45 minutes
Servings: 2 loaves

INGREDIENTS:

- *2 Tablespoons quick rise yeast*
- *4 cups bread flour*
- *1 1/2 teaspoon seasoned salt*
- *3 Tablespoons sugar*
- *2/3 cup baked potatoes, mashed*
- *1 1/2 cup onions, minced*
- *2 large eggs*
- *3 Tablespoons oil*
- *3/4 cup hot water, with a temperature of 115 to 125°F (46 to 51°C)*

DIRECTIONS:

1. Put the liquid ingredients in the pan. Add the dry ingredients, except the yeast. Form a shallow well in the middle using your hand and put the yeast.

2. Place the pan in the machine, close the lid, and turn it on. Select the express bake 80 settings and start the machine.

3. Once the bread is cooked, leave it on a wire rack for 20 minutes or until cooled.

NUTRITION: Calories: 160 Total Carbohydrate: 44 g Total Fat: 2 g Protein: 6 g

20 Spinach Bread

Preparation Time: 2 hours 20 minutes
Cooking time: 40 minutes
Servings: 1 loaf

INGREDIENTS:

- *1 cup water*
- *1 Tablespoon vegetable oil*
- *1/2 cup frozen chopped spinach, thawed and drained*
- *3 cups all-purpose flour*
- *1/2 cup shredded Cheddar cheese*
- *1 teaspoon salt*
- *1 Tablespoon white sugar*
- *1/2 teaspoon ground black pepper*
- *2 1/2 teaspoons active dry yeast*

DIRECTIONS:

1.   Put all the liquid ingredients in the pan. Add all the dry ingredients, except the yeast. Form a shallow hole in the middle of the dry ingredients and place the yeast.

2.   Secure the pan in the machine and close the lid. Choose the basic setting and your desired color of the crust.

3.   Set white bread cycle and Press Start.

4.   Allow the bread to cool before slicing.

NUTRITION: Calories: 121 Carbohydrate: 20.5 g
Total Fat: 2.5 g Protein: 4 g

Preparation Time: 3 hours

Cooking Time: 30 minutes

Servings: 20

INGREDIENTS:

- *3 cups bread flour, sifted*
- *1 tablespoon white sugar*
- *1 tablespoon sunflower oil*
- *1½ teaspoons salt*
- *1½ cups lukewarm water*
- *1 teaspoon active dry yeast*
- *1 cup potatoes, mashed*
- *4 teaspoons crushed rosemary*

DIRECTIONS:

1   Prepare all of the ingredients for your bread and measuring means (a cup, a spoon, kitchen scales).

2   Carefully measure the ingredients into the pan, except the potato and rosemary.

3   Place all of the ingredients into the bread bucket in the right order, following the manual for your bread machine.

4   Close the cover.

5   Select the program of your bread machine to BREAD with FILLINGS and choose the crust color to MEDIUM.

6   Press START.

7   After the signal, add the mashed potato and rosemary to the dough.

8   Wait until the program completes.

9   When done, take the bucket out and let it cool for 5-10 minutes.

10 Shake the loaf from the pan and let cool for 30 minutes on a cooling rack.

11 Slice, serve, and enjoy the taste of fragrant homemade bread.

NUTRITION: Calories: 106 calories; Total Carbohydrate: 21 g Total Fat: 1 g Protein: 2.9 g

22 Zucchini Herbed Bread

Preparation Time: 2 hours 20 minutes
Cooking time: 50 minutes
Servings: 1 loaf

INGREDIENTS:

- ½ cup of water
- 2 teaspoon honey
- 1 tablespoons oil
- ¾ cup zucchini, grated
- ¾ cup whole wheat flour
- 2 cups bread flour
- 1 tablespoon fresh basil, chopped
- 2 teaspoon sesame seeds
- 1 teaspoon salt
- 1½ teaspoon active dry yeast

DIRECTIONS:

1.   Put all of the fixings to your bread machine, carefully following the **DIRECTIONS:** of the manufacturer. Set the program of your bread machine to Basic/White Bread and set crust type to Medium.

2.   Press starts. Wait until the cycle completes. Once the loaf is ready, take the bucket out and let the loaf cool within 5 minutes. Shake the bucket to remove the loaf. Transfer to a cooling rack, slice then serve.

NUTRITION: Calories: 153 Fat: 1 g Carbohydrates: 28 g Protein: 5 g

Nut, Seed and Grain

23 Bagels With Poppy Seeds

Preparation Time: 5 Minutes
Cooking Time: 25 Minutes
Servings: 8

INGREDIENTS:

- *1 cup of warm water*
- *1 1/2 teaspoons salt*
- *Two tablespoons white sugar*
- *cups bread flour*
- *1/4 teaspoons active dry yeast*
- *quarts boiling water*
- *Three tablespoons white sugar*
- *One tablespoon cornmeal*
- *One egg white*
- *Three tablespoons poppy seeds*

DIRECTIONS:

1.   In the bread machine's pan, pour in the water, salt, sugar, flour, and yeast following the order of ingredients suggested by the manufacturer. Choose the Dough setting on the machine.

2.   Once the machine has finished the whole cycle, place the dough on a clean surface covered with a little bit of flour; let it rest. While the dough is resting on the floured surface, put 3 quarts of water in a big pot and let it boil. Add in 3 tablespoons of sugar and mix.

3.   Divide the dough evenly into nine portions and shape each into a small ball. Press down each dough

ball until it is flat. Use your thumb to make a shack in the center of each flattened dough. Increase the whole's size in the center and smoothen out the dough around the whole area by spinning the dough on your thumb or finger. Use a clean cloth to cover the formed bagels and let it sit for 10 minutes.

4.   Cover the bottom part of an ungreased baking sheet evenly with cornmeal. Place the bagels gently into the boiling water. Let it boil for 1 minute and flip it on the other side halfway through. Let the bagels drain quickly on a clean towel. Place the boiled bagels onto the prepared baking sheet. Coat the topmost of each bagel with egg white and top it off with your preferred toppings.

5.   Put the bagels into the preheated 375°F (190°C) oven and bake for 20-25 minutes until it turns nice brown.

NUTRITION: Calories: 50 cal.; Total Fat: 1.3 Total Carbohydrate: 8.8 Protein: 1.4

24 Double Coconut Bread

(Prep time: 10 minutes | Total time: 4 hours 10 minutes)

INGREDIENTS

- *1 egg yolk only*
- *1 cup of unsweetened coconut milk*
- *1 and a half teaspoons of coconut extract*
- *White flour: 3 cups*
- *3⁄4 teaspoon of salt*
- *1 and a half tablespoons of vegetable oil*
- *1⁄3 cup of coconut*
- *1 and a half teaspoons of bread machine yeast*
- *2 and a half tablespoons of sugar*

DIRECTIONS:

1. Add all ingredients to the bread machine in the suggested order by the manufacturer.

2. Select sweet cycle—press start.

3. Serve fresh and enjoy

NUTRITION: Calories: 165 Total Fat: 4g Carbohydrates: 28g Protein: 5g

Preparation Time: 5 Minutes

Cooking Time: 25 Minutes

Servings: 8

INGREDIENTS:

- *1 1/3 cups water*
- *2 Tablespoons butter softened*
- *3 Tablespoons honey*
- *2/3 cups of bread flour*
- *1 teaspoon salt*
- *1 teaspoon active dry yeast*
- *1/2 cup flax seeds*
- *1/2 cup sunflower seeds*

DIRECTIONS:

1. Put all the liquid ingredients in the pan. Add all the dry ingredients, except the yeast. Form a shallow hole in the middle of the dry ingredients and place the yeast.

2. Secure the pan in the machine and close the lid.

3. Set white bread cycle and Press Start.

4. Just in the knead cycle that your machine signals alert sounds, add the sunflower seeds.

5. Allow the bread to cool before slicing.

NUTRITION: Calories: 140   Total Carbohydrate: 22.7 g Protein: 4.2 g Total Fat: 4.2 g

26 Flaxseed Honey Bread

(Prep time: 10 minutes | Total time: 3 hours 40 minutes)

INGREDIENTS

- *Vegetable oil: ¼ cup*
- *1 and a half cup of bread flour*
- *Honey: 3 tablespoons*
- *1 and a half teaspoon of salt*
- *Ground ginger: 1 teaspoon*
- *1 and a half cup of whole wheat flour*
- *1 and a 1/3 cup of lukewarm water*
- *1 and a half teaspoon of instant yeast*
- *Half cup of ground flax seed*

DIRECTIONS:

1. Put all the ingredients in the pan of the bread machine as per the suggested order.
2. Select the basic cycle and medium crust—press start.
3. Check dough. It should not be too sticky or too dry. Add water or flour one tbsp. at a time.
4. Enjoy fresh with butter.

NUTRITION: Calories: 158; Total Fat: 3g; Carbohydrates: 28g; Protein: 6g

27 Honeyed Bulgur Bread

(Prep time: 10 minutes | Total time: 2 hours 10 minutes)

INGREDIENTS

- *2 tbsp. of honey*
- *1/4 cup of extra coarse bulgur wheat*
- *Boiling water: 1/4 cup*
- *1 package of active dry yeast*
- *1 teaspoon of salt*
- *Half cup of bread flour*
- *1 tbsp. of vegetable oil*
- *1 and 1/4 cups of all-purpose flour*
- *3/4 cup of water*
- *1 tablespoon of skim milk*

DIRECTIONS:

1. Add all ingredients to the bread machine in the suggested order by the manufacturer.
2. Select basic cycle and press start.
3. Enjoy fresh.

NUTRITION: Calories: 136; Total Fat: 3g; Carbohydrates: 24g; Protein: 4g

Preparation Time: 5 Minutes
Cooking Time: 25 Minutes
Servings: 8

INGREDIENTS:

- 1 1/8 cups water
- 1 1/2 Tablespoons flaxseed oil
- 3 Tablespoons honey
- 1/2 Tablespoon liquid lecithin
- 3 cups whole wheat flour
- 1/2 cup flax seed
- 2 Tablespoons bread flour
- 3 Tablespoons whey powder
- 1 1/2 teaspoons sea salt
- 2 teaspoons active dry yeast

DIRECTIONS:

1. Put all the liquid ingredients in the pan. Add all the dry ingredients, except the yeast. Form a shallow hole in the middle of the dry ingredients and place the yeast.

2. Secure the pan in the machine and close the lid.

3. Choose the Wheat cycle on the machine and press the Start button to run the machine.

4. Allow the bread to cool before slicing.

NUTRITION: Calories: 174 Protein: 7.1 g Total Fat: 4.9 g Carbohydrate: 30.8 g

Prep Time: 10 Minutes
Cook Time: 3 hours 10 minutes

INGREDIENTS:
Olive oil: 2 tablespoons
Tepid water: 1 cup
Whole wheat bread flour: 1 cup
1/3 cup mixed seeds (pumpkin, sunflower, sesame, linseed, & poppy)
1 teaspoon of salt
1 and a half teaspoons of dried yeast
Sugar: 1 tablespoon
White bread flour: 2 cups

DIRECTIONS:
Add all Ingredients to the bread machine in the suggested order by the manufacturer. Add seeds in the end.
Select white bread cycle—press start.
Check the dough's consistency if it needs more water or flour. Add one tbsp at a time.
Serve fresh.
NUTRITION: Calories: 140 calories; Carbohydrate: 22.7   Protein: 4.2   Fat: 4.2

Preparation Time: 5 Minutes

Cooking Time: 25 Minutes

Servings: 8

INGREDIENTS:

- *1 (.25 ounce) package instant yeast*
- *1 cup of warm water*
- *1/4 cup honey*
- *4 teaspoons vegetable oil*
- *3 cups whole wheat flour*
- *1/4 cup wheat bran (optional)*
- *1 teaspoon salt*
- *1/3 cup sunflower seeds*
- *1/3 cup shelled, toasted, chopped pumpkin seeds*

DIRECTIONS:

1. Put all the liquid ingredients in the pan. Add all the dry ingredients, except the yeast. Form a shallow hole in the middle of the dry ingredients and place the yeast.

2. Secure the pan in the machine and close the lid. Next is setting the machine to the whole wheat setting, then press the start button.

3. You can add the pumpkin and sunflower seeds at the beep if your bread machine has a signal for nuts or fruit.

4.   Allow the bread to cool before slicing.

NUTRITION: Calories: 148   Total Carbohydrate: 24.1 g Protein: 5.1 g Total Fat: 4.8 g

31 Seven Grain Bread

Preparation Time: 5 Minutes
Cooking Time: 25 Minutes
Servings: 8

INGREDIENTS:

- *1 1/3 cups warm water*
- *1 Tablespoon active dry yeast*
- *3 Tablespoons dry milk powder*
- *2 Tablespoons vegetable oil*
- *2 Tablespoons honey*
- *2 teaspoons salt*
- *1 egg*
- *1 cup whole wheat flour*
- *2 1/2 cups bread flour*
- *3/4 cup 7-grain cereal*

DIRECTIONS:

1.   Put all the liquid ingredients in the pan. Add all the dry ingredients, except the yeast. Form a shallow hole in the middle of the dry ingredients and place the yeast.

2.   Secure the pan in the machine and close the lid.

3.   Choose the Whole Wheat Bread cycle on the machine and press the Start button to run the machine.

4.   Allow the bread to cool before slicing.

NUTRITION: Calories: 285   Total Fat: 5.2 g
Carbohydrate: 50.6 g Protein: 9.8 g

32 Toasted Pecan Bread

Prep Time: 10 Minutes
Cook Time: 3 hours 5 minutes

INGREDIENTS:

2 ½ tablespoons of butter
1 1/4 cups of water
½ cup of old-fashioned oatmeal
3 cups bread flour
½ cup chopped pecans
bread machine yeast: 2 teaspoons
Dry milk: 2 tablespoons
Sugar: 3 tablespoons
1 ¼ teaspoons of salt

DIRECTIONS:

Add all Ingredients to the bread machine in the
suggested order by the manufacturer.
Select Grain and light crust. Press start.
Serve fresh.

NUTRITION: Carbs: 18 g Fat: 5 g Protein: 9 g
Calories: 120

Sweet Bread

33 Apple Cider Bread

Preparation Time: 5 Minutes
Cooking Time: 25 Minutes
Servings: 8 slices

INGREDIENTS:

- *1/4 cup milk*
- *Two tablespoons apple cider, at room temperature*
- *Two tablespoons sugar*
- *Four teaspoons melted butter, cooled*
- *One tablespoon honey*
- *1/4 teaspoon salt*
- *2 cups white bread flour*
- *3/4 teaspoons bread machine or instant yeast*
- *2/3 apple, peeled, cored, and finely diced*

DIRECTIONS:

1.   Place the ingredients, except the apple, in your bread machine as recommended by the manufacturer.

2.   Program the machine for Basic/White bread, select light or medium crust, and press Start.

3.   Add the apple when the machine signals or 5 minutes before the last kneading cycle is complete.

4.   When the loaf is done, remove the bucket from the machine.

5.   Let the loaf cool for 5 minutes.

6.   Gently shake the bucket to remove the loaf and turn it out onto a rack to cool.

7.   Ingredient tip: Look for apple cider sweetened and spiced well, so your bread rises nicely.

NUTRITION: Calories: 164 Total Fat: 3g Carbohydrates: 31g Protein: 4g

34 Black Bread

Preparation Time: 5 Minutes
Cooking Time: 25 Minutes
Servings: 8 slices

INGREDIENTS:

- 1/2 cup water
- 1/4 cup brewed coffee, at 80°F to 90°F
- One tablespoon balsamic vinegar
- One tablespoon olive oil
- One tablespoon dark molasses
- 1/2 tablespoon light brown sugar
- 1/2 teaspoon salt
- One teaspoon caraway seed
- Two tablespoons unsweetened cocoa powder
- 1/2 cup dark rye flour
- 11/4 cups white bread flour
- One teaspoon instant yeast

DIRECTIONS:

1. Place the ingredients in your bread machine as recommended by the manufacturer.

2. Program the machine for Whole-Wheat/Whole-Grain bread, select light or medium crust, and press Start.

3. When the loaf is done, remove the bucket from the machine.

4. Let the loaf cool for 5 minutes.

5.   Gently shake the bucket to pick the loaf and turn it out onto a rack to cool.

NUTRITION: Calories: 123 Total Fat: 2g Carbohydrates: 23g Protein: 4g

35 Brownie Bread

Preparation Time: 1 hour 15 minutes
Cooking Time: 50 minutes
Servings: 1 loaf

INGREDIENTS:

- *1 egg*
- *1 egg yolk*
- *1 teaspoon salt*
- *½ cup boiling water*
- *½ cup cocoa powder, unsweetened*
- *½ cup warm water*
- *2 ½ teaspoon Active dry yeast*
- *2 tablespoon Vegetable oil*
- *2 teaspoons White sugar*
- *2/3 cup white sugar*
- *3 cups bread flour*

DIRECTIONS:

1.   Put the cocoa powder in a small bow. Pour boiling water and dissolve the cocoa powder.

2.   Put the warm water, yeast, and the two teaspoon White sugar in another bowl. Dissolve yeast and sugar. Let stand for about 10 minutes, or until the mix is creamy.

3.   Place the cocoa mix, the yeast mix, the flour, the 2/3 cup white sugar, the salt, the vegetable, and the egg in the bread pan. Select basic bread cycle. Press starts.

NUTRITION: Calories: 70 Cal   Fat: 3 g
Carbohydrates:10 g   Protein: 1 g

36 Coffee Cake

(Prep time: 10 minutes | Total time: 3 hours 15 minutes)

INGREDIENTS

- *1 ½ teaspoons of salt*
- *3/4 cup of raisins*
- *Strong brewed coffee: 1 cup (70°-80° F)*
- *Canola oil: 3 tablespoons*
- *Bread flour: 3 cups + 1 tbsp.*
- *1 whole egg, whisked*
- *¼ teaspoon of ground cloves*
- *1 teaspoon of ground cinnamon*
- *¼ teaspoon of ground allspice*
- *Sugar: 3 tablespoons*
- *2 ½ teaspoons of active dry yeast*

DIRECTIONS:

1. Coat raisins with one tbsp. of flour and set it aside.
2. Add all ingredients, except raisins, to the bread machine in the suggested order by the manufacturer.
3. Select basic cycle. Crust color to your liking. Press start.
4. Add raisins at the ingredient signal.
5. Serve fresh bread.

NUTRITION: Cal. 120; Carbohydrate 49.54g Protein 6.46g Fat: 2g

37 Crusty Honey Bread

Preparation Time: 5 Minutes

Cooking Time: 25 Minutes

Servings: 8 slices

INGREDIENTS:

- *2/3 cup water*
- *One tablespoon honey*
- *3/4 tablespoon melted butter, cooled*
- *1/2 teaspoon salt*
- *1 3/4 cups white bread flour*
- *One teaspoon instant yeast*

DIRECTIONS:

1. Place the ingredients in your bread machine as recommended by the manufacturer.

2. Program the vehicle for Basic/White bread, select light or medium crust, and press Start.

3. When the loaf is done, remove the bucket from the machine.

4. Let the loaf cool for 5 minutes.

5. Gently shake the bucket to remove the bread and turn it out onto a rack to cool.

6. Variation tip: Try adding semisweet chocolate chips and butterscotch chips for an unexpected twist on this simple bread. The resulting product will be gilded with the sweetness that gives the plain version a significant face-lift.

NUTRITION: Calories: 119 Total Fat: 1g

Carbohydrates: 24g Protein: 3g

38 Honey Brown Rolls

Preparation Time: 5 Minutes

Cooking Time: 25 Minutes

Servings: 8

INGREDIENTS:

- *1 ½ cups warm water*
- *One tablespoon white sugar*
- *Two tablespoons butter*
- *½ cup honey*
- *2 cups bread flour*
- *1 2/3 cups whole wheat flour*
- *1 tablespoon vital wheat gluten (optional)*
- *1 tablespoon unsweetened cocoa powder*
- *2 teaspoons instant coffee granules*
- *1 teaspoon salt*
- *2 ¼ teaspoons bread machine yeast*
- *2 teaspoons sesame seeds for sprinkling*

(optional)

DIRECTIONS:

- In the bread machine pan, place the water, butter, honey, sugar, whole wheat flour, bread flour, instant coffee granules, cocoa powder, vital wheat gluten, yeast, and salt in the order the manufacturer recommended. Select dough setting, then press Start and wait for the cycle to be completed.

- Transfer the pan with dough from the machine, and prepare warm water to put the pan in (about 32 degrees C, 90 degrees F). Cover the pan using a towel, and allow the bread to rise about 60 minutes until doubled.

• On a floured work surface, turn the dough out, and punch down. Separate into three portions for small loaves or 12 equal parts for rolls. Shape into balls. Prepare a parchment paper-lined baking sheet, and put rolls on. Spread sesame seeds. Wait for it rises in a warm environment, about half of an hour until doubled

• Prepare the oven to 175 degrees C (350 degrees F).

• Spray water inside the preheated oven, and put rolls into the oven right after. Bake for 15 to 20 minutes until light golden brown for rolls. With loaves, bake for 20 to 25 minutes, until they are brown and sound hollow when tapping.

NUTRITION: Calories: 212 calories; Total Fat: 3 Total Carbohydrate: 42.3 Protein: 6

39 Honey Granola Bread

Preparation Time: 5 Minutes
Cooking Time: 25 Minutes
Servings: 8 slices

INGREDIENTS:

- *3/4 cups milk*
- *Two tablespoons honey*
- *One tablespoon butter, melted and cooled*
- *3/4 teaspoons salt*
- *1/2 cup whole-wheat flour*
- *1/2 cup prepared granola, crushed*
- *11/4 cups white bread flour*
- *One teaspoon instant yeast*

DIRECTIONS:

1. Place the ingredients in your bread machine as recommended by the manufacturer.
2. Program the system for Basic/White bread, select light or medium crust, and press Start.
3. When the loaf is done, remove the bucket from the machine.
4. Let the loaf cool for 5 minutes.
5. Gently shake the bucket to remove the loaf and place it out onto a rack to cool.
6. Ingredient tip: Choose granola with no dried fruit because you will be crushing it for this recipe. Dried fruit would create a lumpy mess in the dough, which would wreck the finished loaf texture.

NUTRITION: Calories: 151 Total Fat: 5g
Carbohydrates: 33g Protein: 6g

40 Nectarine Cobbler Bread

Preparation Time: 10 Minutes
Cooking Time: 5 Minutes
Servings: 12 to 16 slices

INGREDIENTS:

*   ½ cup (1 stick) butter, and at room temperature
*   2 eggs, at room temperature
*   1 cup of sugar
*   ¼ cup milk, at room temperature
*   1 teaspoon pure vanilla extract
*   1 cup diced nectarines
*   1 3/4 cups all-purpose flour
*   1 teaspoon baking soda
*   ½ teaspoon salt
*   ½ teaspoon ground nutmeg
*   ¼ teaspoon baking powder

DIRECTIONS:

1.   Place the butter, eggs, sugar, milk, vanilla, and nectarines in your bread machine.

2.   Set the machine for Quick/Rapid bread and press Start.

3.   While the wet ingredients are mixing, stir together the flour, baking soda, salt, nutmeg, and baking powder in a small bowl.

4.   After the first fast mixing has been done and the machine signals, put the dry ingredients.

5. When the loaf is ready, remove the bucket from the machine.
6. Let the loaf cool for 5 minutes.
7. Gently shake the bucket to remove the loaf, then turn it out onto a rack to cool.

NUTRITION: Calories: 218 Total Fat: 9g Carbohydrates: 32g Protein: 3g

(Prep time: 10 minutes | Total time: 4 hours 10 minutes)

INGREDIENTS

- *1 and a half teaspoons of coconut extract*
- *Half cup of pumpkin puree*
- *1 egg yolk only*
- *Half cup of coconut milk, unsweetened*
- *1 and a half tablespoons of olive oil*
- *1/3 cup of coconut*
- *1 and a half teaspoons of bread machine yeast*
- *2 and a half tablespoons of sugar*
- *3 cups of regular flour*
- *3/4 teaspoon of salt*

DIRECTIONS:

1. Place all ingredients into the bread machine in the suggested order by the manufacturer.
2. Select sweet bread cycle. Crust to your liking. Press start.
3. Enjoy fresh bread.

NUTRITION: Calories: 134 Fat: 3.6 g Carbs: 22.4 g Protein: 2.9 g

42 Sour Cream Maple Bread

Preparation Time: 5 Minutes
Cooking Time: 10 Minutes
Servings: 8 slices

INGREDIENTS:

- *6 tablespoons water, at 80°F to 90°F*
- *6 tablespoons sour cream, at room temperature*
- *1 ½ tablespoons of butter, at room temperature*
- *¾ tablespoon maple syrup*
- *½ teaspoon salt*
- *1 3/4 cups white bread flour*
- *1 1/6 teaspoons bread machine yeast*

DIRECTIONS:

1. Place the ingredients in your bread machine
2. Program the machine for Basic/White bread
3. Select light or medium crust, and then press Start Button
4. When the loaf is done, remove the bucket from the machine.
5. Let the loaf cool for 5 minutes.
6. Gently shake the pan to get the loaf and turn it out onto a rack to cool.

NUTRITION: Calories: 149 Total Fat: 4g Carbohydrates: 24g Protein: 4g

43 Vanilla Almond Milk Bread

(Prep time: 10 minutes | Total time: 3 hours 40 minutes)

Ingredients

- Olive oil: 2 tablespoons
- Honey: 2 tablespoons
- Whole wheat flour: 2 cups
- Active dry yeast: 2 and a ¼ teaspoons
- Bread flour: 1 and ¼ cups
- Vanilla almond milk: 1 and ¼ cups
- Vital gluten: 1 tablespoon
- Salt: 1 and a half teaspoons

DIRECTIONS:

1. Add all ingredients to the bread machine in the suggested order by the manufacturer.
2. Select wheat bread cycle. Light crust. Press start.
3. Enjoy.

NUTRITION: Calories: 87 Cal   Fat: 4 g
Carbohydrates:7 g   Protein: 3 g

Breakfast Bread

44 Buttermilk Honey Bread

Preparation Time: 5 minutes
Cooking Time: 3 hours 45 minutes
Servings: 14

INGREDIENTS:

- *½ cup water*
- *¾ cup buttermilk*
- *¼ cup honey*
- *3 Tablespoon butter, softened and cut into pieces*
- *3 cups bread flour*
- *1½ teaspoon salt*
- *2¼ teaspoon yeast (or 1 package)*

DIRECTIONS:

1. Add each ingredient to the bread machine in the order and at the temperature recommended by your bread machine manufacturer.
2. Close the lid, select the basic bread, medium crust setting on your bread machine, and press start.
3. When the bread machine has finished baking, remove the bread and put it on a cooling rack.

NUTRITION: Carbs: 19 g Fat: 1 g Protein: 2 g Calories: 92

Preparation time: 50 minutes

Cooking time: 45 minutes

Servings: 24 rolls

INGREDIENTS:

- *1 cup warm milk*
- *½ cup butter or 1/2 cup margarine, softened*
- *¼ cup sugar*
- *2 eggs*
- *1 ½ teaspoons salt*
- *4 cups bread flour*
- *2 ¼ teaspoons active dry yeast*

DIRECTIONS:

1.   In the bread machine pan, put all ingredients in the order suggested by the manufacturer. Select dough setting. When the cycle is completed, turn dough onto a lightly floured surface.

2.   Divide dough into 24 portions. Shape dough into balls. Place in a greased 13 inch by the 9-inch baking pan.

3.   Wrap the dough, then allow to rise in a warm area for 30-45 minutes. Bake at 350 degrees for 13-16 minutes or until golden brown.

 NUTRITION: Calories: 180 Carbs: 38g

Fat: 2g Protein: 4g

46 Cranberry Orange Breakfast Bread

Preparation Time: 5 minutes
Cooking Time: 3 hours 10 minutes
Servings: 14

INGREDIENTS:

- 1 1/8 cup orange juice
- 2 Tablespoon vegetable oil
- 2 Tablespoon honey
- 3 cups bread flour
- 1 Tablespoon dry milk powder
- ½ teaspoon ground cinnamon
- ½ teaspoon ground allspice
- 1 teaspoon salt
- 1 (.25 ounce) package active dry yeast
- 1 Tablespoon grated orange zest
- 1 cup sweetened dried cranberries
- 1/3 cup chopped walnuts

DIRECTIONS:

1. Add each ingredient to the bread machine in the order and at the temperature recommended by your bread machine manufacturer.

2. Close the lid, select the basic bread, low crust setting on your bread machine, and press start.

3. Add the cranberries and chopped walnuts 5 to 10 minutes before the last kneading cycle ends.

4.   When the bread machine has finished baking, remove the bread and put it on a cooling rack.

NUTRITION: Carbs: 29 g Fat: 2 g Protein: 9 g Calories: 56

47 Cinnamon-Raisin Bread

Preparation Time: 5 minutes

Cooking Time: 3 hours

Servings: 4

INGREDIENTS:

- 1 cup water
- 2 Tablespoon butter, softened
- 3 cups Gold Medal Better for Bread flour
- 3 Tablespoon sugar
- 1½ teaspoon salt
- 1 teaspoon ground cinnamon
- 2½ teaspoon bread machine yeast
- ¾ cup raisins

DIRECTIONS:

1. Add each ingredient except the raisins to the bread machine in the order and at the temperature recommended by your bread machine manufacturer.

2. Close the lid, select the sweet or basic bread, medium crust setting on your bread machine, and press start.

3. Add raisins 10 minutes before the last kneading cycle ends.

4. When the bread machine has finished baking, remove the bread and put it on a cooling rack.

NUTRITION: Carbs: 38 g Fat: 2 g Protein: 4 g Calories: 180

48 Cranberry & Golden Raisin Bread

Preparation time: 5 minutes
Cooking time: 3 hours
Servings: 14

INGREDIENTS:

- *1 1/3 cups water*
- *4 tablespoon sliced butter*
- *3 cups flour*
- *1 cup old fashioned oatmeal*
- *1/3 cup brown sugar*
- *1 teaspoon salt*
- *4 tablespoon dried cranberries*
- *4 tablespoon golden raisins*
- *2 teaspoon bread machine yeast*

DIRECTIONS:

1.   According to the manufacturer's directions, add each ingredient except cranberries and golden raisins to the bread machine one by one.

2.   Close the lid, select the sweet or basic bread, medium crust setting on your bread machine, and press start.

3.   Add the cranberries and golden raisins 5 to 10 minutes before the last kneading cycle ends. When the bread machine has finished baking, remove the bread and put it on a cooling rack.

NUTRITION: Calories: 175 Carbs: 33g Fat: 3g Protein: 4g

49 Chocolate Cherry Bread

Preparation time: 5 minutes

Cooking time: 3 hours

Servings: 14 slices

INGREDIENTS:

- *1 cup milk*
- *1 egg*
- *3 Tbsp water*
- *4 tsp butter*
- *½ tsp almond extract*
- *4 cups bread flour*
- *3 tbsp sugar*
- *1 tsp salt*
- *1¼ tsp active dry yeast*
- *½ cup dried cherries snipped*
- *½ cup semisweet chocolate pieces, chilled*

DIRECTIONS:

1.   Add each ingredient to the bread machine in the order and at the temperature recommended by your bread machine manufacturer.

2.   Close the lid, select the sweet loaf, low crust setting on your bread machine, and press start. When the bread machine has finished baking, remove the bread, and put it on a cooling rack.

NUTRITION: Calories 210 Carbs 23 g   Fat 13 g Protein 3 g

Preparation Time: 5 minutes

Cooking Time: 3 hours 45 minutes

Servings: 14

INGREDIENTS:

- *3 cups white whole wheat flour*
- *½ teaspoon salt*
- *1 cup water*
- *½ cup coconut oil, liquified*
- *4 Tablespoon honey*
- *2½ teaspoon active dry yeast*

DIRECTIONS:

1.   Add each ingredient to the bread machine in the order and at the temperature recommended by your bread machine manufacturer.

2.   Close the lid, select the basic bread, medium crust setting on your bread machine, and press start.

3.   When the bread machine has finished baking, remove the bread and put it on a cooling rack.

NUTRITION: Calories: 60 Carbs: 11 g Fat: 3 g Protein: 1 g

Measurement Conversions

VOLUME EQUIVALENTS (LIQUID)

US STANDARD	US STANDARD (OUNCES)	METRIC (APPROXIMATE)
2 tablespoons	1 fl. oz.	30 mL
¼ cup	2 fl. oz.	60 mL
½ cup	4 fl. oz.	120 mL
1 cup	8 fl. oz.	240 mL
1 ½ cups	12 fl. oz.	355 mL
2 cups or 1 pint	16 fl. oz.	475 mL
4 cups or 1 quart	32 fl. oz.	1 L
1 gallon	128 fl. oz.	4 L

US STANDARD	METRIC (APPROXIMATE)
⅛ teaspoon	0.5 mL
¼ teaspoon	1 mL
½ teaspoon	2 mL
¾ teaspoon	4 mL
1 teaspoon	5 mL
1 tablespoon	15 mL
¼ cup	59 mL
⅓ cup	79 mL
½ cup	118 mL
⅔ cup	156 mL
¾ cup	177 mL
1 cup	235 mL
2 cups or 1 pint	475 mL
3 cups	700 mL
4 cups or 1 quart	1 L

OVEN TEMPERATURES

FAHRENHEIT	CELSIUS (APPROXIMATE)
250°F	120°C
300°F	150°C
325°F	165°C
350°F	180°C
375°F	190°C
400°F	200°C
425°F	220°C
450°F	230°C

WEIGHT EQUIVALENTS

US STANDARD	METRIC (APPROXIMATE)
½ ounce	15 g
1 ounce	30 g
2 ounces	60 g
4 ounces	115 g
8 ounces	225 g
12 ounces	340 g
16 ounces or 1 pound	455 g

CPSIA information can be obtained
at www.ICGtesting.com
Printed in the USA
BVHW011619120721
611731BV00010B/425